How to Analyze Latent Criminals

Dark Psychology

Unconscious urges Malicious Intentions & Deception

Table of Contents

Chapter 1:Theories on Dark Psychology

Dark psychology is a theory that seeks to explain human behavior and the state of the human mind with regards to the urge and tendency for people to prey on one another and sometimes on other living things; deviant behavior with no biological or evolutionary explanation.

Theories behind Predatory Tendencies

When animals prey on one another, for example the lion killing a zebra, the behavior can be explained as a biological phenomenon, where the lion kills the zebra with the purpose of feeding on it. Feeding is a basic necessity for all living things, and so it is understandable that a lion should be prompted to kill a zebra.

In fact, if the lion did not kill the zebra it would have to kill another animal for food for it to continue living. Owing to their biological needs, predators like the lion have heightened senses of sight, hearing, and even smell to enable them hunt down their prey.

Also on the biological aspect of predation, some experts view deviant behavior as being inherited, which means a child can grow into an adult predator because of carrying genes from a predatory parent.

Since predators and their prey share their natural environment, they evolve together, and as the predator continues to sharpen its senses in order to enhance its hunting skills the prey continues to develop better protective skills such as enhanced speed of running and camouflage.

For example, dogs continue to sharpen their sense of smell while skunks, which are among the animal species targeted by dogs, continue to enhance their prowess in squirting their foul-smelling liquid that keeps predators at bay.

For an idea how strong a dog's capacity to detect scents is, human beings have about 2.3% of the smelling capacity dogs have. The biological explanation for this is that while human beings have 5 million receptors in charge of odor detection – referred to as the olfactory receptors – dogs have 220 million of them.

The environment too has a role to play in promoting predatory behavior among people, but the influencing factors are easy to pick out after learning the individual's history.

For example, some people are wired to pick a fight with everyone around them even when they are treated well by those other people, because as children they were victims of abuse from parents, neighbors, schoolmates, or other people.

In short, the theory of evolution and environmental factors have a good explanation for predatory behavior between people and animals, people and plants, animals and plants, and even among animals and plants themselves. Likewise, there is a biological explanation for such predatory tendencies.

Predatory Behavior Reviewed Through Dark Psychology

Dr. Nuccitelli says the human race is the only species that acts in contrast to its own wellbeing and, unfortunately, its survival as well. There is a predatory behavior among people that fails reason under biological, evolutionary and other logical theories, and that is the behavior reviewed under dark psychology.

This behavior lacks purpose and is often a result of psychopathic motivation or deviant drive.

Other times the drive is solely of a psychopathological criminal nature, where the person's only motive is to victimize other people.

People who manifest psychopathic tendencies are considered to have a personality disorder marked with anti-social behavior, and while they, together with the deviants can disrupt normal life for other people, their behavior does not always stretch to criminality.

That is why there is no simple solution to deal with psychopaths and deviants, as compared to criminals whose simple solution is to invoke the law.

The Dark Aspect of People's Consciousness

When the dark aspect of people's consciousness is discussed, what quickly comes to mind is the image of serial murderers and psychopaths, yet there are many human predators that neither kill nor commit sexual assault.

Experts reckon the capacity to victimize others is not exclusively reserved for a few individuals.

In fact, according to Dr. Michael Nuccitelli, a renowned American psychologist, every person has the potential to victimize a fellow human being and even other living things, only that many people restrain themselves from these urges.

Unfortunately, there are other people who act on their underlying impulses and hence the potential to victimize others becomes a reality.

According to Dr. Nuccitelli, the proportion of human predators that get into physical contact with their prey is only 30% and the rest of it constitutes people who victimize others psychologically and emotionally.

Nuccitelli, who is licensed in the state of New York, describes dark psychology as the exploration of people's criminal and cybercriminal minds, as well as their deviant thinking.

In his private consultancy, he gives advice regarding cyber-bullying and cyber-stalking, sexual predation advanced online, personal defamation and corporate denigration carried out over the internet, and on the psychology of cyber and cyber-criminal nature.

He also advises on matters pertaining to creation and maintenance of reputation over the digital platform.

Adler's Theory of Subjective Processing

Although human beings have survival instincts, they also have the basic traits of kindness and compassion, and that is why they are able to filter bad thoughts from good ones as they relate with one another.

Nevertheless, there are those who are not able to keep off what Dr. Nuccitelli terms the 'black hole', because as they process the colors that represent their various thoughts, perceptions and emotions, everything shows up black, and all they feel is venom.

As such, all they can release as they relate with other people is pain and everything evil. Dr. Nuccitelli's premise is greatly informed by Alfred Adler's Theory of Subjective Processing.

Adler was an Austrian psychologist who developed the individual theory, otherwise known as the Adlerian theory, on which individual psychology that he perpetuated is based.

According to Adler, every individual's manner of processing thoughts and perception is unique, which means a group of people can have similar experiences and only one of them turns out to be a deviant.

The first concept under the Adlerian theory is that human beings strive for superiority, and this is because deep down them lingers a sense of inferiority.

Nevertheless, the one concept Nuccitelli relies on most in expounding dark psychology is Adler's second, which holds that people have subjective perception. The greatest significance of this concept lies in the fact that an individual's perception ends up guiding him or her in the fight for superiority.

This means if the person's perception is just a figment of the imagination, this person is bound to act in a manner that is illogical and sometimes perverted.

That is why some people have personalities that make them difficult to work or relate with. At the place of work, for example, if your supervisor has an erroneous subjective perception that you are interested in taking up his job, he is likely to seek opportunities to harass and demean you, even when your performance is good.

In fact, if your performance is exemplary, it may serve to cement this supervisor's perception that you are out to outwit him and get his job; perception that is essentially fictitious.

In this case, the supervisor would be trying to subdue you because he takes his fictitious perception to be reality.

Predatory Behavior is Progressive

The dark side of humans, if unchecked, develops over time, where people continue to victimize others for no purpose, the only feasible explanation being that the mechanism by which they filter their perceptions is distorted.

The filters predators have become so detached from any feelings of remorse that they have no problem laying the blame of victimization on the victims themselves. They reckon the victims are to blame for their naivety otherwise they would have protected themselves.

Over time these deviants hone their predatory skills and it becomes natural for them to act on their thoughts of victimization. They end up entering the black hole Nuccitelli and Adler term the realm of 'dark singularity', where all they experience is venom. By this time, the point at which these individuals are fits what modern criminologists categorize as psychopathy.

According to the experts, individuals whose behavior has reached psychopathic levels are beyond remedy, and so the only direction their predatory tendencies can move is deeper into the dark singularity.

It is no wonder then that several criminals who have been released on parole having served jail time because of crimes they committed end up committing worse crimes before long.

Example of Deteriorating Predatory Behavior

A good example of deteriorating predatory behavior is that of Henry Gaskins, nicknamed 'Pee Wee' as he grew up because of his diminutive size.

The first time he was convicted was because he had assaulted a young girl who had caught him trying to break into her home.

However, after his release from prison, it did not take long for him to commit an even worse crime – rape. He was committed to jail this time around for 8 years after raping a 12 year old girl.

After being released on parole in 1968, it only took him a year to commit a grisly murder. In 1969 he killed a woman who had been hitch hiking and dumped her body in some swamp, but not before torturing her.

Gaskin continued committing murder and evading conviction, and his killing spree only came to an end in 1975 when he was convicted on the confession of his associate in crime. Sadly, the count of people he had murdered by this time had reached or exceeded 90, and this was by his own confession and subsequent investigations.

The Challenge of Rehabilitating a Psychopath

Psychologists equate an attempt to change a psychopath to an attempt at lighting up a black hole using a ray of light. The reality is that the ray of light ends up being consumed by the intense darkness, and hence it has no effect on the thickness of the darkness.

A good number of psychopaths end up being committed to mental institutions or condemned to a lifetime in jail.

This is not surprising considering the great correlation that exists between psychopathy and criminal or simply violent conduct, coupled with the insurmountable challenges of rehabilitating psychopaths.

In fact, according to an FBI report prepared in 2012 by a team led by Dr. Paul Babiak, between 15% and 20% of the more than 2 million prisoners in US jails are actually psychopaths.

Dr. Babiak is both an industrial as well as organizational psychologist, and one of the roles he is famed for is helping company executives identify employees who are most likely psychopaths and guiding them in handling such employees in the least disruptive manner.

The Compulsive Dependency Theory

Although naturally everyone has the dark factor, the vast majority of us hardly activate it for aggression or to perpetuate physical hostilities, and that is generally the reason people are able to live together in harmony.

The greatest advantage is that the dark factor in many people is low, as opposed to the elevated dark factor in psychopaths whose trajectory continues to accelerate towards a dark abyss.

When individuals with the elevated dark factor become a nuisance to society, the law of the land is invoked and the general public is protected.

However, some experts view the growing tendency to victimize other people as resulting from a condition termed 'compulsive dependency'.

During interviews with psychologists, psychopaths have on occasion disclosed their personal observation that their tendency to do evil continues to advance in frequency as time passes.

They have been known to admit that their desire to act on their predatory urges ends up becoming addictive.

This premise held in Dark Psychology has a parallel in cosmology as advanced by scientists like Albert Einstein, where the nearer matter gets to the black hole the faster that mass accelerates, and the more difficult it becomes to divert it from the black hole's immense gravity; as per the universal law of astrophysics.

For psychopaths, the more they manage to capture targeted victims the greater the urge to capture more of them, and the more uncontrollable the urge becomes.

This may explain why they end up being caught even after evading the law for a long time.

In their addictive urge to inflict pain on others, they seem to develop a sense of entitlement owing to their twisted perception, and as reality continues to escape them, they become reckless in their attempts to conceal their perverted behavior.

After all, in their view, the victims only get what they deserve.

In the case of Henry Gaskins, the serial killer, he confessed to having killed individuals who dated from different cultures – white versus black – and expressed no remorse because as far as he was concerned that should not have been happening.

A case in point are the murders he confessed to having committed with three accomplices, of Linda and Jeanette who were of white descent but were rumored to have been dating men from the African-American community.

Apparently, according to Gaskin's twisted sense of reality, he was only trying to avenge the society for a wrong done to it by couples who went against the norm.

This was the same argument he presented as he confessed to killing Doreen Dempsey, a 23yr old white woman who had a daughter with a black man and was 7 months pregnant, and still in relationship with a black man.

Although Dempsey was a family friend and Gaskins had even offered her accommodation before, he felt her relationship with black men was too much and needed to be stopped.

Role of Nature and Nurture in Psychopathy

There has been a continuing debate on where the responsibility for psychopathic behavior lies – whether people become psychopaths because they have been pre-disposed right from birth, or they become so as a result of social and environmental factors.

According to Dr. Mark Dombeck, a clinical psychologist, both nature and nurture can influence the development of psychopathic behavior.

He cites a 2006 research paper originated by three members of staff at three universities – Emory (GA), California at Irvine, and University of South Florida – in which historical abuse was reported to have contributed to the personality disorders in some psychopaths.

Experiences of abuse, therefore, were found to have contributed in the nurturing of the individual in a perverse manner; hence creating the psychopath.

The scholars noted that abuse and other aspects of life had affected several of the inmates leading to their psychopathic behavior, going by the responses they gave in questionnaires that the team presented to them.

On further analysis, the scholars found that these criminals had emotional as well as interpersonal issues. They lacked in empathy and remorse, and other related feelings that would give indication of an emotional connection between them and their victims or even other people.

Interactions with the inmates and the responses they provided in the questionnaires gave glaring signs of impulsivity and diminished self-control on the part of the criminals, and also showed how greatly lacking they were in judgment.

The factors highlighted in the study serve to confirm the basic tenets of Dark Psychology, including the psychopath's propensity to commit evil deeds without an iota of remorse.

Besides physical abuse, there are other social and environmental factors, among them rejection, which can lead to people having their otherwise dormant evil traits emerge.

Ted Bundy, the Necrophile as Example

Ted Bundy was a serial killer who confessed to having murdered 30 girls across seven US states. The fact that he took pride in referring to himself as a cold-hearted 'SOB' goes to underline the non-explainable inclination psychopaths have to inflict pain on other people.

Even during trial, he would look straight at the TV cameras with a bright face and wave, like a celebrity taking in the glamorous limelight.

Heinous as his crimes were, Bundy's perversion may not have been solely a result of bad genes. It is thought his upbringing had a hand in it.

For starters, his mother had for several years masqueraded as his sister, only because she had him out of wedlock at the age of 22 years and his parents wanted to hide the shame.

Later when he learnt the truth about his real mother, he felt betrayed and seems to have held it against her forever.

Moreover, the cousin who had disclosed the secret to him had done so in malice, considering he had proceeded to label him a bastard in his face.

Worse still, Bundy never learnt who his biological father was, yet there was rumor he may have been a product of incest, his violent maternal grandfather having been his father. If this rumor had reached his ears, and with the disappointment he already had from having been lied to by his mother, it may have led him to take it out on the helpless girls he ended up killing.

It is also possible Bundy did not feel much loved as he grew up exposed to different family setups, not because family members did not love him but because he might have found it difficult to open up to them. It seems like he had developed trust issues after that childhood betrayal by his immediate family, and hence did not want to place himself in a position of vulnerability.

Bundy Might Have Felt Unlovable

Ted Bundy had initially been Ted Cowell, having taken the surname of his grandfather, Samuel Cowell.

It was only after his mother, Eleanor Louise Cowell, married a man called Johnny Culpepper Bundy with whom she ended up having four children that Ted adopted the name Bundy.

By this time, Ted had begun to develop a cold attitude towards people, and efforts by Johnny Bundy to show him affection were rejected. He actually had little respect for his step-father.

At the same time, he showed no inclination to bond with either his mother or his step-brothers, and the only person he seemed to care about was his grandfather. It appears he had developed a warped admiration for him.

Nobody seemed safe from Cowell's violence that extended even to the family dog, and it is said that one day he threw his own daughter, an aunt to Bundy, down several stairs because she had erred in oversleeping. Yet all that violence did not deter Bundy from getting close to him.

Instead, Bundy later admitted to having had much respect for his grandfather and having wanted to associate himself with him. This old man that Bundy admired was even a bigot who, for no apparent reason, despised black people and Jews as well as Italians and everyone catholic.

It is worth noting that Bundy began showing an odd interest in tools of violence at a very early age.

It is reported that one morning before he was of school going age his aunt, Julia, had woken up only to find kitchen knives spread all over her bed as her nephew stood at the bed foot with a smile.

Apparently, growing up in an environment full of violence led Bundy to admire violence, while many people would have been repulsed by it. Clearly, environmental factors can affect individuals in different ways.

Another aspect of Bundy's growing up that seems to have contributed significantly to his violent behavior is an addiction he had developed for pornography. This might explain why he targeted girls and young women for sexual violence and subsequent murder.

The Manipulative Trait of Psychopaths

Psychopaths may or may not be violent, but either way they are perversely great at manipulation. They can defraud you while maintaining a straight face. They have even been known to manipulate law enforcement officers when a crime they have been involved in is being investigated.

In the case of one Scott Peterson, who in 2002 was charged with the murder of his wife, Laci, in the state of California, he was said to have provided his own slipper instead of Laci's to guide the sniffer dog in the search for Laci's body. That was, obviously, meant to ensure the dog did not pick up Laci's scent.

Considering the many lies Peterson had told investigators in an attempt to influence the case as he maintained a charming face, experts have concluded he is a psychopath.

In fact, they have equated his lack of remorse to that of Ted Bundy, the serial killer. Robert Ressler, an FBI profiler, labeled Peterson a sociopath, saying sociopaths are great at conning people while wearing false faces.

By the very acts of killing his wife in cold blood and telling lies to his girlfriend, Amber Frey, regarding his marital status, Peterson showed his callous side; and callousness is one of the major traits psychopaths manifest. Scott Peterson was sentenced to death in 2004.

The Purposefulness of Psychopaths

Another characteristic of psychopaths is purposefulness. They contemplate a crime and calculate how to execute it and cover it up, and then they move to carry out their plan with precision.

In the case of Scott Peterson, he seems to have been planning the murder of his wife for the one month he had been dating Ms Frey. At one point he had told her he was yet to find the right woman to marry, while on another occasion he had told her he had had a wife but had died.

Whatever it takes psychopaths to have their purpose fulfilled they do, and so it is not surprising that Scott Peterson, whose aim was to win Amber over as lover, had cried on the single occasion he spoke to her about having lost his wife. The coldness of this lie is chilling considering it is apparent he spoke of his wife's death as he prepared to murder her.

Peterson had kept his cool even in front of cameras for the four months Laci's body was missing, showing how focused he was on having his mission succeed.

Typical of psychopaths, Peterson was emotionally detached from the pain Laci's family was experiencing all through the search for the missing body.

What he must have reveled in was his success in executing his murder plan. He must also have been proud with himself for managing to manipulate everyone into not finding the body or linking him directly to Laci's disappearance.

One thing that you should keep in mind is that although there are several traits shared among violent criminals, not all of them are psychopaths. Conversely, there are psychopaths who cause anguish to other people without being physically aggressive or violent. However, they are all manipulative, cold and with no sense of remorse.

Chapter 2: Criminology

Crime can be analyzed from a social perspective, to see if there are things that happen in society that lure people into crime, make it easy for people to perpetrate crime, or make it more convenient for crime to be perpetuated.

Dynamics of Crime in Society

To find answers to these basic questions, it is important to consider who actually commits crime and the reasons for it, which areas are most prone to crime, and if crime is on the rise or on the decline.

It would also be helpful to understand if the justice system has a role to play in the prevalence of crime, and if so, how? It is also important to understand the role of the police in curbing crime and also how effective policing is in crime prevention.

It may also help to consider the role of punishment and imprisonment in controlling crime, and how every one of the issues mentioned impacts society.

How Exposure to Crime Impacts Minds

It is true that actions are a result of thoughts processed by the mind, and so if a person's thoughts are twisted there is a high chance the person will engage in deviant activities.

This is evident from the case of Ted Bundy who spent his early childhood exposed to domestic violence perpetrated by his grandfather and later got used to watching violent pornography. This exposure must have normalized violence to Bundy so that normalcy in his mind included violent behavior.

This observation can be extended to the environment within which children are brought up in present day. Even in homes where there is no domestic violence, children are exposed to television programs, movies and social media interactions, many a time without supervision or any kind of control.

As such, they have room to watch crime related material that is negatively impactful on a developing mind.

At the end of the day, what passed for abnormal behavior to children and teenagers a few decades ago is now being processed in the minds of these age groups as normal.

In schools there are incidences of bullying among students, sexual predation of students by guardians, and even bullying of teachers by parents; all witnessed by students.

Similar scenarios play out elsewhere including workplaces, and on the streets where demonstrators have often taken looting and destruction of property as their normal way of expressing the magnitude of their grievances.

In short, there is crime in all sectors of society, being more prevalent in some areas than others.

Moreover, the growing market for security personnel, equipment, surveillance gadgets and advertisements is clear indication that society has accepted crime as part of daily living.

Factors that Exacerbate Crime

Although it would be misleading to point at a single factor as the reason crime exists in society, there are some factors that surface in most of the crime prone areas of the country.

Some of the ones researchers have often highlighted include high levels of poverty, unavailability of jobs, unsuitable police policies, and disproportionately large demographic of young people.

People have sometimes pointed at biological factors as being responsible for criminal behavior, seeing that some children born of criminals end up being criminals themselves.

Nevertheless, while this cannot be entirely ruled out, it fails to explain the reason the rate of crime drastically varies from one jurisdiction to another. That is why the societal factors highlighted by researchers are better placed to help in understanding crime rates and how best to control them.

Poverty and Joblessness versus Crime

Statistics have shown there is a direct correlation between levels of poverty and crime.

For example, in cities and smaller urban centers, the rate of crime is often higher in the impoverished areas than in the residential areas where the affluent live.

The Poor Have Little to Lose

Whereas poverty in itself cannot lead to crime, it puts individuals in a position where they feel they have minimal, if anything, to lose in case they are caught.

So even in the adventurous teen age, a youngster from a rich family cannot escape the thoughts of repercussions from the family and stigma from their affluent friends.

On the contrary, extreme poverty can be demeaning, and when people are conscious they are at the bottom of the social ladder they hold the belief they cannot go any lower.

As such, they can easily be lured into petty crime since the word 'stigma' does not have as much weight to them as it has on the affluent.

This is one of the reasons voters put a lot of emphasis on the issue of unemployment when choosing their leaders. They realize that continuous drop in job availability can easily bring about issues of criminality in an otherwise safe neighborhood.

School Dropout Rate is Dangerous

Not surprisingly, schools in poor neighborhoods do not often offer quality education, which means school dropout rates are likely to be higher in these areas.

When the education the young people receive is not sufficient to land them jobs, they turn to their devious behaviors; sometimes for mischief but often to help them plan how to perpetrate crime without getting caught.

Many of the schools in the impoverished areas, just like the rest of the community, lack in role models, and so there are no success stories to give the young people hope.

Instead, what they see on televisions in public places are luxuries that pander to their appetites, and when opportunity avails itself, they have no qualms stealing in order to have a taste of what the rich enjoy.

Incidentally, whereas being caught with stolen goods is normally a shame, flaunting stolen goodies within the extremely poor communities is often marked with heroism.

This is because, just as in the minds of psychopaths, the notion of normalcy among the extremely poor is distorted. This is not to say that poor people are psychopaths.

It is only indication that stealing from the more affluent may not appear offensive to poor people who feel they deserve a better quality of life.

Morality Level versus Crime

Even in poor residential areas there are families that have high moral standards, sometimes because of the family lineage or background of parents and grandparents, or strong religious faith.

This means there are those families known for their notoriety in crime and those that stand out distinctly for being well mannered, even when they are all exposed to the same societal shortcomings.

In some families, children's mischief grows into petty crime in their adolescence and then into felonious crime as adults only because their deviant ways were tolerated within their families. Others are admonished at the slightest sign of rudeness irrespective of the families' financial standing, and so they grow up with the mindset that good manners is a virtue and crime is non-conceivable.

Hence, the perceptions people develop as they grow up end up shaping their notion of right and wrong, which means they influence the way they act later in life.

For example, research has shown that people who were abused in one way or another in their childhood are three times as likely to become abusive adults as people who were never abused.

This is one factor that explains the reason there is a cycle of crime in some homes or in some communities.

Nevertheless, for some individuals, they embrace crime and seek to participate in it in a bid to fit among their peers when they live among associates with deviant behavior. Understanding this concept can help individuals escape the life of crime even when they live in the worst environments.

Crime Triggers and Enhancers

Although there is the inherent quality human beings have to commit crime, there are some factors that often trigger or enhance its manifestation.

If the triggers and enhancers are identified, it is possible to work towards eliminating them and making the environment unsuitable for them to thrive.

For example, if poverty is one such trigger, affirmative action to uplift the poor might reduce the number of criminals emerging from poor communities.

Money as Motivation for Crime

According to the NCJRS, or National Crime Justice Reference Service, money is one factor that provides the motive for people to commit crime.

Since the modern economy is primarily money-based, many people are tempted to steal money in order to meet monetary needs.

However, many people with unfulfilled monetary needs and temptations do not end up stealing. If, for example, there are two people in dire need of money, the one who works closely with people handling cash may end up stealing. This is because the person has more opportunities to steal.

If you have a big urge to steal but do not have an opportunity to actualize your temptation, you end up not committing the crime.

Compared to a receptionist, a cashier is more likely to steal money from her/his place of work because cashiers handle petty cash on a daily basis while receptionists do not. As such, cashiers have ample opportunities to steal from the large quantities of money they handle.

How Money Motivation Triggers Other Crimes

Sometimes people set out to commit one crime but end up committing more in the process.

For example, in July 2019, a man in Philadelphia tried to steal a car while the owner and his wife were inside a store.

If the culprit, Eric Hood, had not been killed by a crowd that helped the car owner nab him, he would have been charged not only with car theft, but also with assault because he assaulted the car owner as he tried to pull him out of the car in a traffic jam.

He would also have been charged with kidnapping, because incidentally, the couple's three children were in the car as Hood was stealing it.

People have also been known to kill others on the streets in order to steal money from them. One reason robbers commit murder is fear of being identified and later reported to the authorities.

Technology as Crime Enhancer

NCJRS notes that advancement in technology has made it easier to commit money-related crimes, and the reason is that it has become easier and more convenient to transact with money or transfer it using technology.

Essentially, therefore, technology has made money an even greater motivation for crime.

For one, a person can steal money through conventional means like pick-pocketing and then launder it by sending it to various destinations electronically, including the bank. Whereas the thief may be known, the prosecution cannot secure a conviction without evidence, and many institutions are yet to upgrade their systems for ease of auditing.

For firms that cannot afford to invest in secure systems, there is room for someone to commit fraud electronically without being detected.

Already some companies and banks have had massive breaches, some of them having been perpetrated or abetted by their own employees.

In cases of big-time fraud, the people stealing do not necessarily do so because they are in dire need of money.

There are mostly other motivations involved. While some succumb to the euphoria of being able to hack systems, others are simply greedy for money and want to keep up with the Joneses.

In short, for crime to be committed, motivation must be accompanied by opportunity.

That is why experts think the fight against crime must be multi-prong, where efforts are made to reduce the factors that serve as motivation for crime as well as those that provide opportunity for crime to take place.

Fortunately, there are many firms, leaders in their respective industries, which have realized the need to become proactive in reducing motivation for theft. They have, therefore, adjusted upwards the salary scales for employees whose role is to deter theft.

Certainly when the job becomes lucrative, the urge to steal from the employer or to facilitate theft diminishes. The thought of gaining some extra dollars by clandestine means becomes far less alluring.

Instead, the employee feels obliged to protect the employer's money and property as if he/she were a shareholder, because that is how much he/she feels valued by the employer.

Good examples can be found among companies engaged in maintenance of security. In Canada, for example, many security firms pay their employees up to $50,000 per year, but when it comes to maintaining cyber security firms are prepared to pay even double that amount.

For example, in recruitment taking place in September/October 2019, KPMG offered to pay up to $89,000 as annual salary for a Cyber Security Manager; Tech Resources Limited, $84,000 for a Cyber Security Analyst; Hatch, up to $110,000 for a Cyber Security Specialist, and Aviva up to $130,000 for the post of Senior Security Manager.

In the meantime, the salary scale for a security officer at the US Department of Energy has gone up to $166,500 per annum. Responsibilities of this officer include implementation of security safeguards and overseeing security matters on a day-to-day basis.

According to the Nevada Mining Association, the salary scale for a security guard can go up to $67,000 per annum, and the employee still has bonuses and other benefits. It is even said some mining companies pay their security guards over $100,000 per annum.

Why Money is a Great Motivation for Crime

Although money is not always the motivation for crime, it still provides great motivation when it comes to 'white-collar' crime.

Crime is described as 'white-collar' when it is motivated by prospects of financial gain and it does not involve violence.

The Federal Bureaus of Investigations or FBI has identified offenses commonly committed alongside white-collar crimes, and they include deceit and concealment as well as abuse of trust.

Whereas many of these offenses may not qualify as felonies or crimes, they are known to cause damage to the societal fabric and to jeopardize people's chances of succeeding in their life-goals.

For example when people steal, they are likely to look guilty even before they are caught, and bosses are not likely to recommend such people for promotion. Promotions normally go to people who look honest, straightforward and confident.

For a person who is overlooked for promotion yet they are efficient at their work, he or she may harbor feelings of hatred against the boss, which could develop a life of its own as motivation to harm that boss.

In the case of the employee who breaks into the office, he cannot help but tell lies at home about his whereabouts, and such lies can end up jeopardizing family relationships.

Unfortunately, with the addictive nature of criminal behavior, the apparently harmless lies can continue and lead to accumulated feelings of distrust on the part of the spouse and other close family members.

Eventually distrust causes marriages to break, and when marriages break children often find themselves without proper guidance and protection.

It is for this reason that children from broken homes are often linked to bad behavior and crime.

A proper review of the situation finds that one money-motivated crime can have a spiral effect that serves to fuel more violent crimes.

Even if the crime initially committed was white-collar, whose motivations are normally to obtain money and property and to position oneself better to take advantage of business opportunities, other crimes may be committed in an attempt to cover the initial crime.

For example, there are cases where people who have committed white-collar crimes have been involved in the execution of other people; often former accomplices.

They do this if they suspect these people might sell them out. It is important to note that criminals expect everyone they collaborate with to adhere to a certain code of behavior, which includes keeping criminal matters confidential among those involved.

Skudda Gang: How Crimes Come in Series

A good example of how one crime can lead to a sequence of crimes is the case of the 'Skudda Gang' that police in Tampa has busted operating from the state of Georgia in the US.

It appears like the initial plan of the gang members was to enrich themselves financially through fraudulent use of credit cards and theft of identity, but they ended up fueling murders of innocent people, including some of their accomplices and potential witnesses.

They have also promoted drug dealing, acquired weapons illegally, and intimidated witnesses to the extent of driving them out of their homes.

Not only do these gang members have money as their motivation, but they also have a twisted perception of what is right and worthy of praise – a typical example of dark psychology.

The gang, whose majority of members is in their 20's, has daringly rapped about the crimes they have committed. They have even opened a music label within Georgia to stamp their clout in the criminal world.

The music label also serves as a cover for gang's ill-gotten riches, even as it gives the members prestige.

In August 2019 after the arrest of nine of the gang members, the police chief in Tampa disclosed that his team has been investigating the gang for 2 years.

This goes to underline the difficulty posed in catching criminals who use modern technology to perpetrate crime.

Among the common white-collar crimes the FBI has discovered include fraud related to securities, fraud affecting corporations, money laundering and embezzlement.

Money as a Basic Ingredient in Many Rituals

Experts in anthropology have established that many of the rituals that take place in modern society require money as a basic ingredient.

Weddings are such examples. Many weddings that are considered beautiful raise the social status of the couples involved, but the entire function will naturally have consumed a lot of money.

As such, young people can be tempted to commit fraud just to get enough money for a wedding.

Psychologists also reckon money serves to promote one's emotional satisfaction, and this is because we live in a money economy and no longer in the subsistence economy.

As long as people your age, people around you or your relatives have money, you will long to have money whether you are jobless or not.

This means even if the state were to provide everything you need you still would not have emotional satisfaction without money.

It is, therefore, not a wonder that the Tampa gang, suspected to comprise 200 members, had its name as "200 Skudda Gang".

In the street lingo, 'skudda' means "let us get it"; essentially meaning get money in any way you can.

Research has shown that even people deemed rich by the general public do not feel rich as long as there are other people in their social circles who are richer than them.

According to Elizabeth Dunn, who is a professor of psychology, rich people acknowledge or deny their richness depending on whom they compare themselves to.

She refers to one study done in the US that indicates that a person in the middle income group can be emotionally satisfied living within a middle-income neighborhood, but if there are marked income inequalities in the state as a whole, the same person may not be as satisfied.

Obviously, having people in the same region with higher income costs the person some emotional satisfaction.

Money as Substitute for Punishment

Since the world economy has become highly monetized, opportunities for crime have also increased.

Expectations would, therefore, be that there would be more people being punished for crime, especially because modern societies are guided by the rule of law.

Unfortunately, there are some provisions in the various laws that enable perpetrators of crime to pay their way out of punishment. In the meantime, those without money end up serving jail sentences.

That is essentially what fines do – keeping those with money out of jail.

Fundamentally, a jail sentence is given as punishment for the crime committed, but asking for a fine as substitute provides a way for affluent individuals to avoid punishment.

The societal justice system, therefore, makes money a great incentive for crime.

In fact, some criminal gangs have survived for decades simply because they have guaranteed their members bailout no matter the amount of money demanded by the courts. They have also assured them their fines would be promptly paid no matter how hefty.

For those whose crimes are not bailable, they are assured of maximum number of appeals and some of the best lawyers available, with money being no obstacle. This kind of scenario makes money extra alluring and easily baits people into crime.

A case in point is the Colombian drug cartel, dubbed the Medellin Cartel, which was led by Pablo Escobar up until the 1990s.

It was established he not only had money to bail out his henchmen and to pay their court fines, but he had also accumulated more than half a billion dollars to finance his escape when he ultimately turned himself in.

Turning himself in was apparently a gimmick arranged with the Colombian authorities to cool international hostilities in mid 1991.

During this period, there had been a lot of pressure on the Colombian government from the international community led by the US to rein in the drug barons and particularly Pablo Escobar, because the operations of the drug cartels had had negative effects all over the globe.

In fact it is reported that the Medellin gang, which had tentacles not only in other South American countries but also the US, Canada and Europe, raked in around US$60 million in daily profits from the sale of drugs.

Power as Motivation for Crime

There is a lot more criminal organizations do with money, including corrupting the same officers charged with maintaining the law.

Escobar: Example of Power Motivated Crimes

In the case of Escobar, it is said he continued to manage his clandestine operations from behind bars, well facilitated by the prison wardens he had compromised using the money incentive.

His massive financial resources are also the reason he was able to plan his escape as he was being transferred from his Envigado confinement, the jail where he was sent to after he gave himself up, to a jail manned by the military.

Escobar is still a good example of how power can serve as motivation for crime.

He is said to have been responsible for the bombing of the Avianca Plane as it took off from Bogota in November 1989.

Although the criminal act ended up causing the deaths of innocent civilians including two Americans who had taken the local flight, the target had been members of his rival gang and suspected informants.

Even with the knowledge that the flight would have over 100 people on board, Escobar's psychopathic detachment from the feelings of other people led him to plan the bombing just to safeguard his superiority among fellow drug dealers.

It is for the same reason of self-preservation that he set aside a big portion of his gang's drug money to use for his own survival, and there are several incidences that show his strategy worked.

For starters, he was able to control his gang members from the confines of Envigado.

This was mainly because he had access to massive amounts of money to entice the prison guards, who ended up giving him access to telephone and fax facilities as well as radio transmitters as he wished.

In fact, official reports showed he had received over three hundred clandestine visits at the jail within the first three months of his incarceration. His mode of operation ensured no gang member emerged as a substitute leader in his absence.

It is even said that in a bid to safeguard his position as gang leader, Escobar had masterminded the kidnapping and murder of a dozen of his gang members whom he felt had strong leadership qualities.

As for two of his lead drug traffickers named Galeano and Moncada, he is said to have summoned them, still from jail, and he made them know they were going to survive only because of his leniency.

He also let them know that he not only deserved their respect and loyalty but also an increased portion of profits.

When they refused to raise his portion to US$200,000 for every shipment of drugs, he ordered them murdered alongside people close to them including brothers and bodyguards.

Certainly the people killed alongside the two drug traffickers had no influence over the amount of profits Escobar received from the Medellin gang.

This means the reason he ordered them killed was to send a message to the rest of the gang that he was still in power and in-charge of the gang's operations, and that his word should be taken as the law.

Escobar also ordered the murder of two other people who served as leaders in their own cocaine dealing families. Such an act would send a message to his rivals not to cross the line he had set just because he was in confinement.

Clearly, although Pablo Escobar was swimming in drug money, the desire to remain in power in the underground world motivated him to commit heinous crimes irrespective of the relationships he had with the victims.

Gacy: Example of Power Motivated Crimes

Wayne Gacy was convicted of 33 murders for which he received 21 life sentences and 12 death penalties depending on the law that existed in his state of Illinois in the respective periods when he committed the crimes.

Having been brought up by an abusive father who beat him and his sister at a whim, he must have internalized such torturous beatings as a means to manifest power. In fact, at some point in his childhood he had ceased to cry from the beatings probably in defiance.

As an adult, Gacy sadistically tortured his victims before sexually abusing them and then killing them. He mostly targeted young boys whose ages ranged from nine to twenty years.

Although he might have wished to kill them to ensure they did not report him of assault, it is also likely he wanted to prove to himself he had power to subdue them the same way his father had subdued him.

From another perspective, one can see Gacy's view of the world as represented by the neighbors who knew of his father's abusive tendencies and never intervened.

As a grown up, he might have been thrilled to know the agony he was causing the neighborhoods of his victims, especially knowing they could not fight back due to his anonymity.

He now had more power than the one his father yielded when he beat him and his sister mercilessly, and that in itself must have given him satisfaction and motivated him to commit even more crimes.

Fight against Crime and Privacy

It is easy and more convenient to commit money-related crime digitally. It is also easy to trace the perpetrators of such crimes through audit trails.

However, where such crime has not been perpetrated by corporate insiders, the issue of privacy becomes a hindrance.

For example, a bank cannot go releasing people's bank information without their consent, and getting such consent often involves a long process and a lot of hurdles.

Usually a court of law would be involved and it would require some concrete evidence before being persuaded of the need to violate a person's privacy.

So, even if the use of cash is finally eliminated in favor of credit cards and electronic money transfers, the issue of personal rights would still pose a problem in tracing fraudsters.

In short, even if it is apparent anonymous electronic money exchanges provide an enabling environment for behavior of a criminal nature, the need to enhance privacy and respect for individual freedoms is bound to continue to be a challenge in the fight against crime.

Solidarity and Code among Criminals

Besides the money motivation, criminal activities continue to thrive because of the brotherhood that exists among criminals.

Criminals usually look out for one another and send warning signs when they detect trouble close by; where trouble to criminals is in form of law enforcement officers or suspected informants.

Sometimes such brotherhood is enforced through unwritten rules. For example, any member of a criminal gang who snitches on another or the group in general faces the wrath of his colleagues.

In order to serve as an example to others not to be sell-outs, such a member can either be physically tortured or even killed as others watch.

Usually when enforcing the law among gang members, the head of the gang often prefers the most inhumane of methods so as to show his power. It gives him prestige to know there is talk among the group members about his 'cruelty'.

Revenge as Motivation for Crime

There are other varying motivations for crime, a common one being revenge.

Within the period beginning 1940 to 1956, a man by the name George Metesky caused terror by planting bombs at indiscriminate public places within the city of New York.

This psychopathic criminal who was nicknamed 'mad bomber' even before he was caught ended up planting 33 bombs in telephone booths, train stations, libraries and theatres, and such other public places.

Owing to Metesky's twisted perception, he had chosen to cause pain to the public as revenge against his former employer, Consolidated Edison, because the company had denied him disability claim after sustaining an injury while on duty.

Even in recent years, there have been cases of criminals holding members of the public hostage in a bid to seek revenge against people clearly unrelated to the victims.

In 2004, for example, schoolchildren and their teachers were taken hostage by Chechen militants.

The crime against the elementary school in Beslan, a town in Russia, was perpetrated in a bid to coerce the Russian government into withdrawing its troops from Chechnya.

The fact that the militants allowed the standoff to continue for three agonizing days even knowing quite well the majority of their hostages were vulnerable children, shows they were prepared to sacrifice innocent lives just to retaliate against Russia.

It is so far clear that understanding criminals requires dismantling of complex processes, especially after noting how a single crime with its own motive can trigger a series of others that end up overlapping.

Also, the fact that at some point motives of continuing crimes begin to overlap, like in the case of the 200 Skudda Gang, makes it difficult to solve crimes by following their motives.

Nevertheless, with well trained personnel and adequate resources, most crimes can be tackled to their logical conclusion. It is also possible for governments to work through multi-sectoral teams to make crime unattractive.

Chapter 3: How to spot latent criminals

Criminals are normally turned over to law enforcement officers and thereafter taken through the due process, which often culminates with the criminals serving jail term.

Unfortunately there are those criminals who manage to perpetrate crimes without being caught, and sometimes not even being detected. These are the ones referred to as latent criminals, and in some cases they can be more dangerous than the known criminals. Sometimes the crimes they commit do not come to light until much later.

Owing to the stealth of latent criminals, it is not easy to provide a reasonable estimate of their number within any given location. In contrast, it is easy to tell the number of known criminals in an area at any given time because there are statistics within the criminal judicial system.

This awareness makes it easy for deterrent measures to be put in place, and also to catch up with the criminals when they manage to commit crime.

Sociopaths as Latent Criminals

Sociopaths are not easily identifiable, and therefore they can remain as latent criminals for many years.

For one, they are great manipulators. They can charm everyone around them, not only their potential and actual victims, but also those charged with preventing and discovering crime.

According to Kimberly Hershenson, a therapist from New York City, sociopaths can manipulate even the way you dress and the people you associate with without raising any suspicions. This is very common in family relationships where an abusive spouse never gets to face the law.

Sociopaths can charm you into getting what they want while at the same time taking every opportunity to blame you for anything that goes wrong. They are also known to twist their victims' words in a bid to deflect attention from themselves as possible perpetrators of crime.

In the case of Larry Nassar, the US doctor who abused several young gymnasts over the years, one of his accusers, Maggie Nichols, said he had groomed her for abuse over Facebook, where he kept giving her compliments about her appearance.

Unfortunately, a number of latent criminals remain undetected because there is an enabling environment. In the case of Nasser, his crimes thrived because the environment within which the gymnasts trained was conducive for oppression.

According to some victims, the couple that ran the training camps for the US team, Béla and Márta Károlyi, made the environment 'emotionally abusive', and so the vulnerable gymnasts dared not report the abusive doctor.

There are also times when the crimes are known but for some reason the victims or those close to them are not willing to report them.

Sometimes cases fall under the category of latent crimes even when the crimes and their perpetrators are known, only because the cases are handled by law enforcement officers who are incompetent or when there are shortcomings in the judicial system.

According to a 2019 report by The Guardian, the number of rape cases inaccurately recorded by police run into thousands. Obviously such inaccuracies provide a basis for the police not to pursue legal measures, and for the cases that are prosecuted, the inaccuracies provide grounds for them to be thrown out by the courts.

There are also instances when victims of crime fail to report crimes against them because of intimidation from the perpetrators or fear of ridicule.

In some communities, victims face ridicule when they report crimes such as rape by neighbors, and so many choose not to report even after they have been hurt.

Also in some jurisdictions, police officers do not take such cases seriously. One Seokhee Yoon, in his approved Doctorate research report in Criminal Justice, indicates there is skepticism within the police force as well as the judicial system, but when it comes to influencing victims not to report crimes, police skepticism has greater impact.

It has also been established that there are more unreported cases in some crime categories than others. This is probably because for some crimes the victims are less likely to be believed.

For example, people reporting they have been robbed are more likely to be believed than people reporting they have been sexually molested. Hence latent criminality is less in theft than in assault. The lower the level of latent criminality the more accurate the results of analyses done on crime, and consequently the more effective are the measures put in place for prevention of the same.

One way to reduce the incidence of latent crime is to learn how to spot different kinds of criminals.

For example, by knowing how to identify a sociopath, you become better placed to prevent potential crimes or to catch the perpetrator than when you harbor assumptions as to what a sociopath looks like.

One assumption many people make that the behavior of a sociopath reflects that of a scary serial murderer is incorrect. Whereas serial murderers are certainly sociopathic, there are other sociopaths who do not commit murder but cause havoc to people's lives in other ways.

For example, you could have co-workers or neighbors whose thinking is dominated by dark perceptions; and such people are capable of ruining careers and personal relationships. They know how to manipulate people while causing emotional pain to others.

Some research has shown that among twenty-five Americans there is at least one sociopath. This means there is a big chance of having a sociopath among the people you interact with.

It is important to note that several characteristics found in sociopaths are also present in psychopaths.

Characteristics of a Sociopath

Sociopaths are commanding

Sociopaths have superficial charm and intelligence. This means they are not genuinely charming or intelligent, but they fake those qualities so that they can be accepted in positions of leadership.

Once in leadership, they have a good opportunity to manipulate people for their own gain. You need to observe if the so-called leader is trying to command too much attention, because the aspect of commanding attention, according to Dr. Dabney, is used by sociopaths to divert attention from the harm they are actually doing; equating it to the magician's cape.

Good examples of sociopaths who use this characteristic effectively are leaders of religious cults.

Sociopaths are cold

Sociopaths can rationalize their repulsive acts without shame or empathy, and you can tell when a person's feelings are not emotionally moved by an incident that touches everyone else.

According to Adriane Raine, a neuroscientist, the pre-frontal cortex of sociopaths has fewer of the cells responsible for feelings and judgment compared to normal people.

This is the reason they manifest minimal if any empathy and minimal or no respect for ethics. When they hurt other people, they have no sense of remorse. Instead, witnessing other people's pain makes them even more inclined to inflict more of it.

Punishment does not serve as a deterrent for crime as far as sociopaths are concerned, and so if a person is a repeat offender despite the threat of punishment, it is reasonable that they be interrogated like any other suspect every time a crime is committed. This is because sociopaths do not correct their behavior just because they have been jailed in the past for similar crimes.

Sociopaths are hardly nervous

In many cases, individuals give themselves away after committing an offense just by how nervous they become. However, in the case of sociopaths, they rarely show nervousness. They are also not averse to risk.

This goes to show why you should not be quick to eliminate individuals as possible suspects when investigating a crime, just because they are behaving normally and even participating in discussions about the crime committed.

Sociopaths are pathological liars

Sociopaths seem to believe that if they repeat a lie over and over again it will turn into the truth. This should not be surprising once you remember how twisted the perception of a sociopath is, just like that of a psychopath.

Sociopaths like to be in a position of influence, and so they use lies, distortions and manipulation to get to the lead.

They have no sense of shame as they run away from facts laid bare before them, and when they dismiss these facts they do so with great contempt.

You should, therefore, take it as a red flag when you find someone dismissing facts outright without allowing anyone a chance to interrogate them.

For sociopaths, lying is not confined to situations where they stand to gain financially, but rather extends to many other situations; like in personal and other relationships. In all cases, the sociopath's tendency to blame the victim should be noted.

Challenges Posed by Emerging Crimes

Technology has been advancing at a very fast pace, and the effect of globalization is now being felt. This means it is now easy to learn about countries far off from your own, to communicate with the people there, and also to transact business with them. Whereas such advancement brings progress faster than ever before, it also introduces crimes never known before.

For example, human trafficking was generally considered to have ended with the abolition of slavery, but today crimes of human trafficking are on the rise. One reason is that it is easy for sociopathic criminals to seek markets undetected using modern communication technology such as the internet and the mobile phone.

Another reason is that with the exponential economic growth facilitated by modern technology, there are also increasing economic disparities among communities. Coupled with the civil wars that have affected some countries in Africa, Asia and Latin America, poverty levels have drastically risen in some communities. This has made some people very vulnerable, and it is not unusual for adults to traffic children related to them.

Criminals also have a sound opportunity to kidnap and traffic children from their own neighborhoods. This is only possible because there are affluent criminals willing to pay for trafficked children, and with increased access to flights across the world, distance is no longer an issue.

Another reason is that there is room for such trafficked victims to be used as tools for criminal activity such as pornography. Perpetrators of such crimes are motivated by financial gains, because there is lucrative online business for pornography.

It is also now easy to exploit poor families, who fall prey to the deviousness of criminals who promise them jobs abroad only to end up using them in brothels or on farms in conditions of slavery.

In short, old crimes are re-emerging because conditions have become more conducive to perpetrate them, and new ones are being devised as people seek to pander to their dark side for prosperity, fame or cruelty.

To curtail the incidences of such crimes, everyone involved in maintenance of law and order, including police officers, the judiciary and legislators need to be literate in technology to a reasonable level. This would help legislators understand cyber crimes better as they legislate on how to curb them, and the police to catch cyber criminals with relative ease.

The general public also needs to be educated on how to protect themselves and their children against technology related crimes, and other crimes that are part of cyber-crimes such as kidnapping.

Chapter 4: Body Language

Some of the signs you read from the body language of a criminal are linked to the fact that criminals do not feel emotions the normal way other people do particularly if they are psychopathic.

Some signs are also linked to the sense of aggression that many criminals experience that makes them hunger to harm other people.

For criminals who are also psychopathic, the signs they manifest in body language reflect their general lack of conscience. In any case, they neither recognize nor appreciate the morality standards against which normal people gauge their actions.

Studies have shown that it is possible to detect psychopaths through their behavior because when you engage them in conversation, the way they respond both verbally and by body language is subtly different from other people.

Subtle Differences in How Psychopaths Communicate

Next you are going to see some patterns that can give you an indication you are dealing with a psychopath, but which you can only detect if you are keen.

Speaking in past tense

Using past tense when discussing an ongoing event or one likely to happen is odd, yet it is one of the characteristics of psychopaths.

A good example is the statement, 'But I thought people were allowed to do that', when speaking of something that people have just been asked not to do. Someone else would normally say, 'But I think people are allowed to do that'.

In a brain storming session where people are advised not to do something, participants would be speaking in the present tense because they want to find a solution to the current situation.

Experts have not found a good explanation why psychopaths have the tendency to use the past tense in such situations, but their suspicion is that because psychopaths are normally able to detach themselves from their actions, the use of past tense aids in setting the environment to a distant time; away from the reality of the present time. Being detached from their environment

Psychopaths also have the tendency to detach themselves from the environment they are in, the reason for instance their behavior does not correspond to sad situations like everyone else around.

A case in point is the March 2017 horrific incident where Randall Coffland, a 48 year old man from Illinois in the US killed his two teenage daughters and then proceeded to call 911 after shooting his wife who had just called 911. In her call, the wife is clearly distraught and is even unable to give directions to their physical address.

On the other hand, the man's call is methodical with no emotions whatsoever. He plainly declares he has shot his two kids and his wife, and that the next thing he was going to do was shoot himself.

When asked about his physical address, he avoids answering the question and simply repeats that he was going to kill himself as well. He does not want to dwell too long on the environment he is in owing to his actions, and so he says only what he had planned to say and nothing helpful to the 911 operator.

Using distracting body language

You are often warned not to believe everything a psychopath says because they are deceptive and often say things to try and make themselves appear good. That is why you may wish to rely on a person's body language to know if he/she is being sincere or not. Unfortunately, the manipulators that psychopaths are, they have learnt to manifest body language that can be misleading.

In the case of one Robert Pickton, he kept making elaborate gestures with his hands often throwing them into the air, when answering even the simplest of questions during an interview with police detectives.

Pickton was a criminal psychopath who was convicted of murdering 6 women after having been on trial for 26 murders, and at one time he bragged to an undercover agent that he had had a target number of fifty murders.

There are some telltale physical signs that detectives look for when interviewing a suspect, like looking away to avoid the detectives' eyes or making a snarl in contempt, but when a suspect throws his hands around haphazardly the way Pickton did, it becomes difficult for the detectives to decipher.

Feigning convincing charm

Studies have shown that it is usual for psychopaths to engage freely in conversation and to use words that express emotion, but this is not because they feel any of the emotions they speak about.

Rather, it is because they hunger for attention and want to be admired. So, they tell you what, in their view, is likely to impress you. In short, psychopaths often say what is deemed to be the right thing at the appropriate moment in order to play on your emotions.

Speaking in a controlled manner

Criminals never want to make mistakes that can make them caught, and when they are psychopathic, they are even more meticulous. Unlike other people who get animated when they mention words that portray emotions, psychopaths speak calmly and also quietly, and in a manner that is controlled.

Experts think this is a deliberate effort to control how they interact with other individuals.

Obviously, people who have nothing to hide are not afraid of getting carried away in their emotional state, but criminals are cautious not to embrace emotions in case they end up revealing too much for their own good.

This is clear in the video where Chris Watt who murdered his wife and two young children in August 2018 answered media questions in a calm and controlled fashion. Barely 24 hours into committing the murders, Watt was able to respond to questions posed by Tomas Hoppough, a journalist from Denver 7's, in a calm and controlled manner.

Language meant to justify

When something horrific happens, such as murder, you would expect everyone to express emotions of sadness, anger, and probably fear. However, a psychopathic criminal does not express such emotions, but instead analyzes the same scenario in the language of cause versus effect.

That is why instead of acknowledging it was wrong to assault a victim, a psychopath finds it alright to say, 'She asked for it', or 'She provoked me'.

On the contrary, people who end up killing others inadvertently or in self-defense cannot be caught using such language. Instead they are overwhelmed with emotion and often require professional counseling to salvage their sanity.

Focusing on basic requirements

Psychopaths have no inclination to discuss matters of either an emotional or even spiritual nature, but they would rather discuss basic physical needs. For example, when talking about the events that transpired on the day of a particular crime, a psychopathic criminal often focuses on personal requirements such as the food he/she ate and the game he/she played, or even the money that was at stake.

They hardly say anything that shows they realize the impact their behavior has had on the other person.

Talking a lot about self

Psychopaths are known to speak a lot about their achievements, and when they are not trying to portray themselves as heroic, they play victim. The ultimate goal for them is to draw other people's attention for various reasons.

One of the reasons is that they want to feel important, and that is why some psychopaths have become serial killers to revel in media attention as they escape capture.

Another reason for seeking attention is to gain people's trust and ultimately to manipulate those people into seeing them as victims.

Playing victim can be as simple as pretending to be lost in the city or in a rural setting, so as to have the trusting person offer to show them the way. This gives the psychopath an opportunity to harm their trusting victim.

If everyone were to learn how to identify criminals and more so psychopathic ones through their body language, these criminals would have fewer chances of succeeding in committing crime.

Skilled law enforcement officers would also find it easy to identify culprits from a range of suspects when a crime has been committed.

How Criminals Avoid Detection

There are often telltale signs of a guilty person when you speak to him/her, and they include looking away as you speak to them to avoid direct eye contact.

However, many psychopaths are aware of those telltale signs and they consciously avoid manifesting them so that they do not give themselves away.

Luckily, experts in criminology know that this behavior that is meant to counter the norm is likely to happen, and so they have also learnt to look for signs of someone trying too hard not to show signs of guilt.

Traci Brown, an expert in body language, has broken down the mannerisms of Chris Watt as he responded to questions during the media interview with Denver 7's. Chris Watt had murdered his wife towards dawn on her return from a business trip, and then when he went to dispose of her body he took their two daughters with him and murdered them as well.

Betraying Body Language

Traci Brown watched the video from Denver 7's where their journalist interviewed Chris Watt, and she identified a number of telltale signs that indicated Chris Watt was not entirely innocent.

Swaying the body

First of all, Brown observes that Chris Watt keeps swaying his body around as the interview continues. That is a way of the criminal's body impulsively signalling he wants to leave the scene the soonest possible, because it is threatening his cover.

Nevertheless, since Watt knows he is better off telling the media the story of his wife's and children's disappearance in his own version, he makes a conscious effort to stay. He wants to make use of this opportunity to manipulate the thinking of the media and public.

Hugging oneself

The expert says when Chris Watt hugs himself as he has done for most of the interview it is a sign that he is anxious. He may think that nobody is likely to link the disappearance of his wife and children to him, but he cannot be certain.

Hugging himself is a way of trying to tame that anxiety and to remain calm. What is not certain is whether he sub-consciously fears he might say the wrong thing and be caught, or the presence of a TV camera is the reason for his anxiety.

Cracking a tiny smile

When Watt is asked a question that does not threaten his cover as the unknown criminal, a tiny smile emerges from his mouth in a rather spontaneous manner. This is because he is excited about that particular question.

His body system responds by manifesting joy at what he believes is being able to get away with the crime, as indicated by the direction the questioning is taking. In the video, that minute smile has surfaced a number of times and that is indication Watt is pleased with the particular questions and considers them safe for him.

A good example is when the journalist asks him early on in the interview what he thinks might have happened to his wife. He is happy to be given the leeway to tell the version of the story he wants people to believe, and he is hopeful that by telling that version he will be able to escape suspicion.

He unconsciously cracks a tiny smile and takes the opportunity to dramatize concern, explaining how the previous night he had hoped the kids would come running into the house.

Incidentally, he speaks in monotone and his emotions are unchanged and that should raise an eyebrow.

When asked about his relationship with his kids, Watt gets some more relief and smiles as he says they are his life. He seems to relish the question and proceeds to explain how he chats with them at dinner. He actually gives a pictorial description of what he says to them regarding what to eat or not eat; how he watches them curl on their couches, and such other minor details.

That behaviour should concern you as a person curious about Chris Watt's behavior because no matter the motive of the questioning, usually a normal person who has lost his closest family members within less than 48 hours cannot afford to smile when discussing the topic unless there is indication they are safe and sound.

What is the relief that makes Watt crack a smile when discussing the unfortunate incident? What makes him take pleasure in explaining their experience at table while nobody has any idea what the fate of those same kids are?

That is a tell-tale sign worth pursuing. An expert in body language can tell that Watt is relieved to have the topic switched from explaining the events of the fateful night to talking about mundane things like how he and the kids relate. Yet the events of that night are more likely to help reveal what happened to Watt's wife and kids.

A contemptuous smile

Psychopaths delight in showing contempt towards other people. They are spiteful and want to feel superior to others. Contrary to the old belief that psychopaths are incapable of emotions, an expert psychologist from the Netherlands, Carlo Garofalo, says it is the positive emotions that psychopaths do not elicit, but they are great at expressing negative emotions such as anger and aggression, which give them contemptuous gratification.

When the journalist from Denver 7's asks Chris Watt what he thought of his wife's situation, like if he thought she would survive, he responds with a snarl. Although there is nothing suspicious in what he says about not wanting to draw conclusions, his body language seems to challenge the journalist's audacity to ask a question that suggested he might have an idea what had transpired.

The psychopath always wants to lead and influence other people's thinking, but when the journalist asks a probing question Watt feels slighted at having to explain himself; hence that smile often described as being asymmetrical. The snarl is a show of contempt for the question and it happens in a spontaneous manner, and it does not correspond to the words he utters because those are calculated – "saying he wishes his wife and kids would come back immediately."

Sticking out the tongue a little

Chris Watt is angry at his wife probably because like any other psychopath he blames his victim for his current situation; of the anxiety he is feeling as he goes through the questioning process. This can be seen by the way he sticks out his tongue, albeit slightly, when his wife is mentioned.

When he is asked to explain what had happened in the last moments before his wife's disappearance, Watt sticks out his tongue a little before proceeding to answer how she had come back from a business trip at 2am. Again, when asked what his wife's name is, he says 'Shanann', and again his tongue spontaneously sticks out a little; the same indication that any mention of his wife was provoking him into anger though he tried to conceal it.

This act happens also after Watt has spelled his children's names to the journalist, which means he is angry at all his victims for apparently causing him trouble. As is usual with psychopaths, they deem their victims guilty of inviting the harm that befalls them, which means by extension they are guilty of the trouble the perpetrator has gotten into with the police and everyone else.

When all these signs, or a number of them, are combined, they indicate the person involved is restless and uncomfortable about the situation. In fact, in the case of Chris Watt, he confessed to having murdered his expectant wife and their two daughters one day after the interview with the Denver 7's journalist.

It is the expert's view that although psychopaths can manipulate people through what they say; they are not able to entirely manipulate their body language. As such, you need to learn the tell-tale signs of a psychopathic criminal in order to decipher them.

Manipulation is prevalent in every sphere of life, and because not everyone who is manipulative is out to hurt you, what you need to look out for are those manipulators with malicious intentions.

For you to be successful in whatever agenda you have, you need the skills to influence people, which in many cases fall under the bracket of persuasion.

Persuasion may appear like manipulation because your intention is to succeed in getting your listener(s) to see things your way, but it actually differs in that you intend both of you to benefit at the end of the process. On the contrary, people who manipulate others intend to benefit at the expense of those other people.

An uncle who persuades his niece to go shopping with him wants to strengthen the bond they share as relatives, but a rapist who lures a young girl into a store and buys her snacks before driving off and having his way with her will have manipulated her into thinking his friendliness was genuine.

If, for example, you are a political candidate trying to influence supporters of another candidate to vote for you instead, you may find yourself engaging tactics of persuasion. Such persuasion does not particularly harm anyone but only intensifies competition, and so you need not worry about it.

This chapter will dwell on how to avoid manipulation of a predatory nature, the one people with psychopathic tendencies employ for their twisted gratification.

Workplace Manipulators

It is important to keep in mind that a workforce comprises people from different communities, and the same case applies to the political class.

The same is applicable to the clergy and any other group you can think of. In short, as long as there are manipulators in the general society, you will find manipulators in every other group.

Manipulators at your place of work may have different approaches from those found within the political class, but fundamentally they apply the same principles of deception, intimidation and other negative behavior that make them stand out as being insensitive.

At the workplace, for example, you may find a
co-worker trying to bully you into doing tasks
that are not in your job description or tricking
you into thinking those tasks are part of your
responsibilities. You may even have a
manipulative boss who makes you feel like you
are always performing below par, just to justify
his/her failure to recommend you for a
promotion or a pay rise.

In politics, a politician may alienate an opponent
from the voters by unashamedly igniting and
spreading propaganda that portrays that
opponent as untrustworthy. The malicious
message may, for example, be that the candidate
amassed his wealth by swindling poor people
through a pyramid scheme.

A politician who fails to clinch an elective post
due to voters' manipulation by a psychopathic
competitor gets hurt just as much as an
employee who stagnates in his/her career due to
a boss with psychopathic tendencies.

For that reason, you can apply the same skills to avoid manipulation irrespective of where your psychopathic manipulators are. It is important that you employ the skills you learn consistently, not just because consistency makes them effective, but also because this way you end up cultivating an image of a person who is not vulnerable to manipulation.

In short, you will avoid being the go-to person whenever a psychopathic manipulator wants to satisfy his/her twisted desires. Manipulators have a talent for identifying vulnerable people and making them easy targets, and once you are consistently a victim of manipulation your self-confidence begins to wane.

Unfortunately, even people who empathize with you may not be available to help you through life, and so you can end up with a ruined career or social life and generally lead a miserable life unless you learn to protect yourself.

Best Way to Guard against Manipulation

The skills you are going to learn here are meant to help you confront your manipulators head-on.

If you can do this, manipulators know straightaway you are not the easy target they initially thought you were.

One great thing about these skills is that you can use them effectively irrespective of whether you are lower or higher in the social, economic, or other strata compared to the manipulator.

Even in instances where you will not have managed to deter a manipulator from trying to influence you, at least you will have asserted yourself and taken control of the situation as you will soon see.

On the contrary, when you are not equipped with skills suitable to deal with manipulators, you end up succumbing to manipulation and often suffering quietly – which is what eats into your self-confidence.

Once you have skillfully taken control of your situation, you can easily devise a plan that suits you in the long-term. If, for instance, you have to deal with a psychopathic boss on a day-to-day basis, you can choose to take up an advanced course that will make you more marketable, and hopefully in a few years' time you can secure a job in a different company.

Do not embrace excessive special attention

Attention may be healthy and even preferable, but not all of it is good. You need to note when attention is becoming a little excessive.

Manipulators work towards establishing a relationship with you first and to win your confidence, so that you get to believe they are your allies in all circumstances.

Once you have become confidantes, it is normal to drop your guard and to allow the person into your life, letting him/her learn what your vulnerabilities are. Such a person also gets to learn how much he/she can benefit from manipulating you.

Of course for psychopathic manipulators the gains may not matter much, since what mainly gives them the thrill is activating their dark side and hurting other people whether it is emotionally, financially, physically or otherwise.

If a manipulator tests the waters and finds you sophisticated or confident, he/she is likely to leave you alone or at least become less enthusiastic to bait you into a trap.

During the testing period, manipulators assess how eager you are to please and how easily you succumb to shaming. Then they capitalize on these vulnerabilities.

Study a person before opening up

You need to take note when an influential colleague or one who is career-wise superior to you takes great interest in you.

Whereas people are sometimes naturally drawn to each other, you need to make a deliberate effort to find out about a person who tries to become close to you, especially if that person is out of your league.

If you learn that the person is associated with suspicious behavior, be bold enough to give indication you are not enthusiastic about becoming close to that person.

Example: Harvey Weinstein's Manipulation

In the case of the movie mogul, Harvey Weinstein, who in 2017 was first accused of sexually abusing women in the industry, there are some actresses who could have avoided abuse if only they had asked around about him.

Instead, they were blinded by their eagerness to thrive in the industry, and by extension, to appear worthy in Weinstein's eyes and they failed to see the predator's trap.

Resist Being Put Down

You may not hinder a manipulative person from saying demeaning things to you, but you can refuse to take their word seriously.

You should be on the lookout for people who attempt to make you feel below par in your work performance, in beauty, or in any other way that would hurt or shame the average person.

Any person who is genuine in trying to forge a friendship with you will not in any way utter something that makes you feel awful about yourself or that puts you down.

Psychopaths use this strategy of making you feel inadequate or of little worth so that when they subsequently ask you to do something that favors them, you find yourself wishing to accomplish it in order to prove to them that you are not worthless after all.

If it is something you are not comfortable doing, such a person is likely to put some pressure on you; sometimes stressing how cowardly you are if you do not do it. Learn to dismiss such negative sentiments.

Anyone who puts you down or blackmails you does not have your welfare at heart and is out to manipulate and misuse you.

Example: Psychopathic Manipulation in the office

Suppose you are a petty cashier and your boss calls you in the morning and asks you to give him/her $200 refundable by the end of the day.

If you carry the money and simply hand it over, you will be liable for misuse of company money if the boss fails to refund it as promised.

That is why you need to be bold enough to take a payment voucher with you and make the boss sign it before you can hand over the money. If not an official payment voucher, have the recipient write something down to show he/she has received the money.

The fact that the boss will have signed for the money will prompt him/her to refund it even if the initial intention was to swindle you.

Many employees have lost their jobs because of fraud perpetrated by their bosses, only because those employees did not deter psychopathic manipulation from the onset.

Example: Volkswagen 'Dieselgate'

In 2015 when the US discovered the Volkswagen Group was exporting vehicles to the country that did not meet the standards set by the EPA but whose software showed they did, the company began to fire software engineers and other employees said to have taken part in the cheating.

According to a 2015 report by Newsweek, Volkswagen released 11 million vehicles with the 'cheat software' into the market at global level, and half a million of those went to the US market.

As Congresswoman Janice Danoff Schakowsky observed when the company CEO, Michael Horn, was being questioned by the Energy and Commerce Committee, it is unfathomable that a big company would miss the chance to patent a unique innovation made by its employees.

The insinuation here is that the fact that Volkswagen did not make an attempt to patent the 'unique' technology meant the executives knew their engineers had no new technology but merely used software to beat the US EPA pollution checking systems.

In 2004, the EPA set the minimum pollution levels allowed for diesel vehicles. All other vehicle manufacturers gave up trying to enter the US market when it became clear that if they had to attain such low levels of pollution then those vehicles would not be commercially viable.

In short, top executives and managers at Volkswagen put pressure on engineers to deliver the impossible but when the cheating was discovered they threw the engineers under the bus; behavior that is typical of psychopathic manipulators.

Ferdinand Dudenhöffer, who has served as director at Duisburg-Essen University's Center for Automotive Research, told Newsweek that the culture at Volkswagen has been autocratic, where employees are put under pressure to deliver results irrespective of the means.

He gave an example of instances where an employee would be instructed to look for a solution to a problem, and then he would be subtly told that in case he could not manage the company could always find a more capable engineer.

Such is the behavior of manipulators, who use coercion and intimidation while making it look like everything is up to you.

Sometimes when things go wrong, it takes very long for other people to realize you are just a victim of manipulation and not the culprit, and so it is up to you to protect yourself so that you do not fall prey to manipulation.

In the Volkswagen case, it has taken around three years for some top manipulators to be discovered. Towards the end of 2018, Volkswagen fired Rupert Stadler who at the time of the scandal served as an executive at Audi, for the role he played in the cheating and cover-up. Audi AG is a subsidiary of the Volkswagen Group.

While the public generally considers psychopaths to be heartless criminals who deserve long jail-terms, medical and legal professionals have their different views that are at times in conflict.

The media enhances the public view by portraying criminal psychopaths as the epitome of evil for committing crimes of extreme violence in cold blood while showing no remorse when caught.

Legal Position on Psychopaths

Defense lawyers have often tried to argue that their clients are mentally unstable, citing the fact that psychopathic behavior is considered in psychology to be a medical condition.

This means these psychopathic criminals should not be held responsible for their actions. The lawyers claim insanity as their strongest defense, so that the court can discharge their clients or have their sentences commuted.

However, it is not always easy to prove that the psychopath's impulsivity was beyond his/her control, and so many of these criminals end up being handled like anyone else in court.

Why Psychopaths Are Criminally Responsible

Some scholars argue that it is not reasonable to hold psychopaths morally responsible since the neurological disorder they suffer from prevents them from understanding moral issues.

While this sounds logical, other scholars find the inference these scholars make that because psychopaths cannot be held morally responsible they also cannot be held criminally responsible to be erroneous.

The reason is that psychopaths understand quite well that their criminal actions have dire consequences, and that is why they even make attempts to avoid being caught.

In short, it is justifiable to hold psychopaths criminally responsible even as they are exonerated from moral responsibility, and it is also fair to subject them to the full force of the law like any other criminal.

Experts who believe that psychopaths should be held responsible for their criminal behavior explain that if a person understands that laws on crime exist and how they work, then he/she qualifies to be subjected to those laws.

They reckon it is immaterial that the same person does not understand the moral reason behind those laws.

While it is reasonable to subject psychopathic criminals to the law of the land because they understand the consequences of their criminal acts, it remains a challenge how to correct their behavior, considering history has proven that imprisonment does not deter such people from committing more crime.

How to Change Psychopathic Criminal Behavior

So far no treatment has been found effective for psychopathy, especially because there is no medication that can begin to elicit empathy from individuals who do not already have it.

Psychopaths do not conform to social norms, and in spite of all the punishment meted in jail and the counseling provided, psychopathic criminals continue to commit grave crimes at will after their release.

Still, scholars have not given up seeking solutions for the disturbing behavior of psychopaths, and one such scholar is Dr. Kent Kiehl, a psychologist who has specialized in psychopathy and served at the University of Mexico.

In 2012, Dr. Kiehl established that the amount of gray matter within a psychopath's paralimbic brain system is less than in other people.

In short, the difference between a psychopath and other people is of a biological nature, and the psychopath's shortcoming in the brain makes him/her unremorseful and also anti-social.

It saddened Dr. Kiehl to note that although he had made an important discovery about the deficiency in the brains of psychopaths, he had no solution to it.

Fortunately, there were other experts in Wisconsin at the same time who were trying to seek a solution to the problem of rehabilitating psychopathic criminals, and they had embraced a progressive approach.

The Decompression Model

These health professionals did a study within the Mendota Juvenile Treatment Center or MJTC, where they avoided the use of stringent deterrent measures and punishment at the facility; a very unconventional way of handling juveniles.

The subjects of this study were the youth with the worst criminal behavior at the institution.

The experts reasoned that since the behavior of psychopaths is hardly corrected through punishment, it may be helpful to try a different method that does not result in the vicious cycle of indiscipline-punishment-defiance and more indiscipline.

In any case, it has been established that the chances of a psychopath committing fresh crime after being released from jail compared to any other criminal are 6:1, showing that harsh punishment could be making the problem even worse.

According to Kiehl, by the time the youth were admitted at MJTC, other facilities had found them uncontrollable with the average youth having more than twelve formal charges already filed.

The decompression model worked through positive reinforcement, where the youth under study were monitored on a continuous basis by members of staff to see if there was any sign the youth behaved better than before even to the minutest degree.

Any improvement in behavior was rewarded as a form of reinforcement, meaning the reward was meant to encourage the person to continue behaving in that positive manner.

The subjects of study were also informed that they would receive better rewards as they continued to behave well, and so those whose good behavior continued for longer periods received greater prizes. The rewarding began with candy bars then graduated to permission to enjoy video games, to more alluring offers.

According to the experts carrying out the study, the idea was to let the youths experience the basic advantages of fitting into society.

Dr. Kiehl observed that the reward system MJTC used was derived from neuroscience, particularly considering that studies done using brain scans have indicated that people's learning center within the brain responds positively to food as well as video games.

Relative Success of the Decompression Model

The subjects of the MJTC Decompression Model were monitored for five continuous years, even for those who were discharged from the institution before the end of the 5 year duration.

Dr. Kiehl terms the results 'staggering' because while 64% of the youths under the study were re-arrested within a period of 4 years, the percentage of those re-arrested from the youth not treated under the Decompression Model was a whopping 98%.

Kiehl explains that to mean that the rate of recidivism was reduced by 34% under the program at the MJTC.

Moreover, none of the youths from the program committed any homicide unlike others who committed murder after they had been released. Those under the program were actually found to have only a 50% likelihood of committing crimes of a violent nature.

Psychopathic Behavior Change through the MJTC Programs

Dr. Kiehl was interested in learning whether the Decompression Model ended up stimulating the brain in a manner to produce more grey matter within the psychopath's paralimbic system. After all, it has already been noted that normal people have greater amounts of gray matter in that brain area than psychopaths.

That is why he sent some brain scanners to MJTC in 2012 to try and establish if the brains of the inmates were affected in any way by the model that used positive reinforcement and no harsh punishment.

Studies are still continuing, with Dr. Kiehl's team having already carried out a study of about 4,000 criminals comprising juveniles and also adults who are known to have committed violent crimes.

In another program at MJTC referred to as 'Today=Tomorrow Program', Dr. Kiehl and his colleagues have been trying to treat youths under study by targeting cognitive behavior. Here they train them to appreciate the link between their own thoughts, emotions and even attitudes to the way they behave.

On the overall, these experts try to establish the reason the youths have a problem with their thought process, and then they try to help them think responsibly with a view to enhancing their social skills.

The Douglas County Juvenile Department Study

The success of the Today=Tomorrow program was evident when youths from the Douglas County Juvenile Department in the state of Wisconsin were put under study. The rate of recidivism among 48 of them dropped by 85% within a year, and within two years with the sample being reduced to 12 youths the recidivism rate dropped by 94%.

While no conclusive medical or behavioral solution has been found to treat psychopathic criminals, Dr. Kiehl continues to work with neuroscientists to try and identify the specific areas of the brain that need to be targeted for treatment in order to improve behavior and reduce impulsivity in committing crime.

Dr. Kiehl has committed himself to scanning his subjects' brains three rounds in the course of treatment, with a view to observing the possible changes in their brains as they continue to undergo the behavioral treatment.

The programs carried out by experts based at the MJRC and the Douglas County Juvenile Department are aimed at finding preventative solutions to the problem of psychopathic crime.

If, and when found, the jails will have far fewer inmates than they have today because it will be possible to reduce the rate of recidivism among psychopathic criminals.

How to Prevent Children from Becoming Psychopaths

There are a good number of cases where psychopathic criminals are found to have had troubled childhood, and health experts have been trying to see if there is a way that children can be prevented from becoming psychopathic themselves.

Ted Bundy, for example, spent his early childhood with his violent grandfather, and he ended up becoming a psychopathic murderer.

Wayne Gacy is another psychopathic killer who grew up in an abusive home where his father was violent and unreasonable.

Experts in mental health therefore see a correlation between children's exposure to adversity and children growing up to become unemotional and callous adolescents.

Some experts did a study at Tulane University, which was based on children growing up in foster homes.

The findings, which were published in the 'American Academy of Child and Adolescent Psychiatry, indicated that it is possible to intervene in the lives of children exposed to harsh environments, so that in the end the behavior that is normally a precursor to psychopathic tendencies is pre-empted.

Study on Romanian Orphans

During the early years of the 2000s, there were many orphans still neglected in orphanages in Romania following the fall of the communist government of dictator, Nicolae Ceausescu.

As people from the West continued to rescue those children, experts took the chance to carry out some research on the effects of hardship on behavior.

Half of a group of toddlers rescued from Romanian orphanages was put under foster care of great quality while the rest were held in institutions, and they were all observed by researchers as they grew up.

When the children reached the age of 12 years, the researchers, who worked under a project dubbed 'Bucharest Early Intervention', found that compared to children who grew up in normal homes, those in orphanages manifested serious callousness and traits devoid of emotions.

The researchers included Dr. C. H. Zeanah of Tulane and Nathan Fox of the University of Maryland, as well as C. A. Nelson of Harvard Medical School.

These experts established that the children who as toddlers had received quality attention from their caregivers were able to express empathy as adolescents, unlike their counterparts who were neglected or had insensitive caregivers.

According to renowned author, Kathryn Humphreys, who has done research on the mental health of infants at Tulane, children can be molded to develop good behavior by regulating the behavior of their caregivers.

This means that by insisting that caregivers be sensitive to children and their needs, children who would otherwise have become violent psychopaths can grow up with empathy and good behavior.

Both the researchers and author Humphreys concur that one effective intervention for children with potential to become psychopaths is to ensure the caregivers are responsive to the needs of the children under their care.

Violent Recidivism: Prison Aggression Inconclusive

In considering the inmates qualified for parole, the authorities take into account the number of incidences the prisoner has shown aggression during the period of incarceration.

It is believed that prisoners who are constantly violent in prison are likely to also become violent in the community once released from prison. However, this reasoning has been put to question through various experiments.

One study involved 148 male inmates, all adult and convicted of violent crimes, with their behavior being monitored before and after their release from prison.

At the end of the study, it was found that manifestation of excessive aggression in prison is no indication that the individual is incapable of changing behavior to one of non-aggression once released from prison.

Conversely minimal aggression in prison is not a signal that the individual is unlikely to be violent out of prison.

According to the researchers, it is possible some inmates become excessively aggressive due to the nasty environment they find themselves in, or because they find it hard to adapt to life in prison.

Among the 148 criminals under the study, those whose records showed they had been aggressive in prison three occasions or more ended up being charged with violence more times after being released from prison, and even sooner than the ex-convicts who had no record of violence while in prison.

In the meantime, the criminals whose incidences of prison aggression did not exceed two did not show significant risk of going back to violent crime.

From these findings, it is easy to conclude that the repeated aggressive behavior observed under the institutional environment is a sign the culprit is likely to continue the behavior outside the institution.

This is actually the conclusion the researchers arrived at after taking other pertinent factors into account, including the age and ethnicity of the ex-convict and the duration the individual had stayed in prison.

Nevertheless, other observations made in the same study introduced doubts into the reliability of the above findings. For one, there were some ex-convicts whose prison records showed they had been violent up to three times or even more, yet they were never involved in acts of violence once released from prison.

At the same time, there were individuals released from prison with a record of non-violence, yet they were sued for acts of violence after they had been released from prison.

As such, the long-held belief that an inmate's aggressive behavior is a reflection of how he/she is bound to behave on release from prison is not air-tight.

In order to bring down violence-related recidivism, more research needs to be done with a view to finding better means of evaluating prisoner behavior, because that would break down the complexity of rehabilitating ex-convicts.

Role of Prison on Psychopaths

It is said the US has the highest rate of incarceration the world over, with federal prisons taking in one prisoner every one and a half minutes.

There are different reasons for imprisoning wrongdoers, one of them being to carry out justice for those who have been wronged while meting punishment on the offending party.

Prison Positives

One other important reason for incarceration is to keep the rest of the community safe, especially where violent criminals are concerned. Experts in the field of criminology refer to this effect as 'incapacitation'.

In the meantime, debate rages on regarding whether imprisonment really helps to reduce the rate of crime in society.

Proponents of incarceration have cited harsh prison conditions that anyone would wish to keep away from. They believe that someone who has served prison time may do his/her best to consciously avoid crime so as not to undergo the terrible prison experience already known to him/her.

Another positive impact prisons have on inmates is rehabilitation from drugs and even alcohol, for those who came in as addicts. They are able to enjoy free counseling, treatment and education, and so when their prison term is up they are able to face the world soberly and to process what is good for them with relative clarity.

Prison Negatives

People who speak against imprisonment of criminals reckon incarceration has potential to increase the rate of crime in society.

One aspect of prison life they cite as a bad influence is the same one that proponents of incarceration consider positive – the harsh environment within prison.

Instead of it being a deterrent, they see it as having a negative effect on the mental health of inmates, and for those who already have mental issues the environment makes them worse.

This means that for a cold blooded murderer, imprisonment may have the effect of making him even colder in the execution of his crimes.

The conditions in prison are also largely blamed for the aggression that many ex-convicts manifest, traits that begin while they are still under incarceration.

Inside prison is where many convicts develop cynicism against the judicial system, becoming distrustful of it.

As such, they are not mentally prepared to correct the behavior that led them into incarceration, and so they end up developing a casual attitude towards the law.

Another negative aspect of imprisonment is that inmates are kept away from relatives and close friends once incarcerated, yet those are the people who would be relied upon to help the same inmates integrate well into society once they are released.

For this reason, ex-convicts end up being alienated from the rest of the society, and with that they sense stigmatization and dislike.

Not surprisingly, such people are likely to commit offenses against members of their community without any feeling of remorse.

After all, the same alienation that the judicial system began while the ex-convicts were prisoners continues to make them feel like unwelcome outsiders.

Such alienation coupled with lack of gainful employment increases the risk of violent recidivism, because the ex-convicts are tempted to steal, and they are likely to do it using violence.

Chapter 7: Multi-Pronged Approach to Disarming Predators

This chapter concludes the book, and it is an attempt to provide the way forward with regards to mitigating the damage done by predators.

While it would be great to speak of a solution in curbing predatory behavior, research findings show that experts are still struggling to identify a program, be it a social or a scientific one, which can effectively change the behavior of predators at the core.

The studies being pursued by experts like Dr. Kiehl and others highlighted in the book are good examples.

Even religious people who believe prayer is a panacea for all problems are not sitting on their laurels when it comes to eliminating psychopathic criminal behavior.

In fact, experts in sociology like Professor Byron R. Johnson have indicated that the effect of religion in preventing crime cannot be ruled out, and that the correlation should be studied further.

The best way forward, therefore, is to utilize the means available for now to minimize the potential for psychopaths to cause damage.

The Elusive Predator

Some predators are dangerously elusive, yet they keep hurting other people.

The problem is that it is difficult to prove a case against them as the offenses they commit do not meet the criteria for litigation. In fact, their manner of offending makes it difficult for anyone to build a case that is air-tight whether it is at work, within the social environment, or anywhere else.

So, these psychopaths continue their predatory behavior, knowing quite well that any complaints lodged against them can only result in their word against that of their accusers.

While they are emboldened by the knowledge they cannot be sued or punished for their behavior, some things they do can be so injurious as to lead other people into depression or even suicide.

Such behavior is common at the workplace, where employees with psychopathic tendencies continue to suppress others as they unjustly take credit for workplace successes. Others just bully their targets in devious ways for no apparent reason.

Shed Light on Non-Violent Psychopathic Behavior

As pointed out by Dr. Nucitteli, the subjective behavior of predators is often erroneous, and because they have a misplaced sense of self-worth, they seek to assert their superiority in a manner that hurts other people.

One way their harmful effect can be mitigated is to continue shedding light on their existence, and to let normal people understand that the vindictiveness of psychopaths is unjustified.

With this knowledge, potential victims, for example at the workplace, can easily brush off any attempted intimidation from psychopaths, hence safeguarding their own mental health.

It is estimated that 1% of the general population is psychopathic, and behavioral scientists have found, as reported in 'Behavioral Sciences & the Law' journal, that among the most successful businesspeople, 3% of them have psychopathic tendencies.

Since psychopaths who do not end up in jail for criminal offenses continue to live among normal people, you are likely to encounter one or more of them in your daily life.

Sadly, psychopaths who spend a lot of time with you like at the workplace can end up making your life torturous. Their condition is often described as a 'sub-clinical psychological disorder', where their behavior does not explicitly portray them as psychopathic while in actual fact it has a devastating effect on their victims.

In some disciplines like politics and history, characters like these are described as being Machiavellian in their manipulation, because they become nasty to others as they pursue their goals, all the while ensuring they do not leave behind any trail.

The term 'Machiavellian' is used to indicate that one can do anything, no matter how unpleasant, to achieve his/her end-goal. In fact, people who are Machiavellian are notorious for being devious and without any morals.

The best way to deal with sadistic people with such underhand behavior is to be your own guard, especially because those who try to report them to people in authority are often seen as petty.

In any case, oftentimes the psychopath is a person in a position of authority, with capacity to influence the outcome of your complaint. In the meantime, he/she shows no remorse as you hurt.

As noted by a Harvard Medical School psychiatry professor, Ronald Schouten, psychopaths do not let conscience or empathy obliterate their goal of succeeding at the expense of other people.

This is not surprising because such emotions do not exist in psychopaths. Their egocentric nature keeps them focused on their anticipated gains, irrespective of how short-lived those gains may be or how likely it is that other people are going to get hurt.

Communicate Clearly and Firmly

The reason clear communication is helpful is that you let your psychopathic colleague know you are not naïve. That way you are likely to shake their confidence and discourage them from making you their target of manipulation.

One way to make your communication to a psychopathic colleague effective is to set firm boundaries. Psychopaths loathe boundaries and once you have set these the psychopath is bound to test them like a child does.

Consider those boundaries to be your protection and stand your ground when the psychopath tries to test them.

If, for instance, a psychopathic workmate asks you to perform chores that are known to be his/her responsibility, make it clear you are not prepared to do them as you only have sufficient time to carry out your own duties.

Such a person may attempt to manipulate you, making you feel awful about your refusal or even powerless to resist. Stand your ground. It is important to remember that you always have a choice to say no whenever you are not comfortable with something another person suggests.

For you not to become the easiest target for people with psychopathic tendencies, it is important that you are consistent in safeguarding your boundaries.

If the psychopath is relentless in pursuing you, one of the helpful options you have is to physically leave the environment.

If you are physically close to the individual, you can take a walk, visit the wash room, or just fake some urgency to attend to something else.

If the psychopath is texting you or communicating online, you can opt to block him/her. The idea is to give yourself a breather; time to evaluate the situation and to see what your best options are.

Once you have had your break and can think clearly, ensure you do not return to the psychopath's toxic environment again.

Even if the person offers you a ride, politely turn it down because when a psychopath begins putting pressure on you it marks the beginning of abuse.

Keep Calm

You also have the option of informing the person in clear terms that you find them irrational in their request, but as you do so you need to be calm and to use a controlled tone. Alternatively, you can inform them you are not comfortable having the discussion right then.

Do not succumb to the fear of being seen as rude, because psychopaths will always view assertiveness as an unwelcome challenge to them.

It is important to note that psychopaths can be relentless in their pursuit in a manner that can provoke you, and so you need to disengage, if not physically step aside, in order to prepare yourself emotionally.

You need to keep your cool and to show no signs of frustration, such as cracking your knuckles or grinding your teeth, because that would be a sign of success on the part of the psychopath.

The more a psychopath sees you cracking under his/her pressure the more he/she is determined to pursue you. In short, the non-verbal communication you manifest is just as important as the words you speak to the psychopath.

Since psychopaths are not rational, it is a waste of time to try and reason with them. That is why asserting yourself is a better idea the way you would when dealing with a child. The only difference is that you need to be careful not to appear condescending.

If you enter into an argument with a psychopath and he/she concedes to seeing things your way, very likely the person will be buying time to re-strategize. Usually the aim is to deceive you into putting your guard down, and when you are in that phase of false security the person strikes.

This is the time you find yourself giving them something you had held onto because you knew the person did not deserve it, or generally breaking your protective boundaries.

Often the risk of such manipulation is high when it comes from people who have been close to you in one way or another, such as co-workers, family members or ex-lovers. This is because they know your vulnerabilities and can easily capitalize on them without a care when they are psychopathic.

You might, for example, find yourself consenting to sitting in for such a person at work as he/she takes leave of absence that you know to be unnecessary. In the meantime, your work schedule gets messed up and you have to put in extra hours that you had not planned for.

For an ex-spouse, you might find yourself accepting to drop off kids that you co-parent when it is his/her responsibility to pick them up from your place, turning it into a habit that disorganizes your plans and hurts your feelings.

Any time you find yourself becoming closer than you should with a psychopath, remind yourself to 'disconnect', even if it means reciting this word like a mantra.

Remain Focused

Since psychopaths are great liars as well, they would do anything to keep you from catching their lies.

One of their effective tactics is distraction, where they use gestures in a rather elaborate manner. Other times they keep touching you as they speak or staring you down.

There are even times when they deliberately stand so close to you as to cause discomfort.

As you follow the psychopaths' hand gestures or think of how to handle the uncomfortable position they have put you in, it becomes difficult for you to pick out any contradictions in what they say, or anything that does not sound right.

You ought to remember that psychopaths always try to sound more knowledgeable, intelligent, and accomplished than they really are.

They also know that without engaging the diversionary tactics, you can easily catch their blatant lies and probably call them out.

Keeping your focus is important because you can follow every word these psychopaths say, and also have an opportunity to ask questions. If they change the topic as they are likely to do when they are caught lying, it will confirm to you that they had ill intentions and you just managed to protect yourself from falling victim.

Identify Psychopathic Traits

The very nature of psychopathic behavior means there are professions likely to attract or even accommodate more psychopaths than others.

These are professions where competition to reach the top is ruthless, whether such ruthlessness is outright encouraged or just ignored. Even geographically, there are some areas that seem to have more psychopaths than others.

As pointed out by Robert Hare in his publication, 'Snakes in Suits', there is at least one individual who is psychopathic in every one - hundred people sampled from the public in general.

Jon Ronson, who authored 'The Psychopath Test: A Journey through the Madness Industry', narrowed research to the business sector where he found that 4% of people leading in business, including CEO's, are psychopaths.

Here next are subtle signs to look for in identifying a psychopath in your daily life.

Deceptive Charm

When psychopaths make you feel special, as charm is one of their most common characteristics, it is easy for you to relax and to let them take control of things.

People are often won over by psychopaths even when the issues at stake affect their own lives, because psychopaths are adept at blindsiding their victims.

Dr. Igor Galynker points out that people have the tendency to promote and elect psychopaths, without realizing they actually intend to position themselves strategically to be able to accomplish something that is self-serving.

The Full Disclosure tactic

Often psychopaths volunteer information of a personal nature without much prodding, or any at all, and their intention is to bait you into reciprocating.

This means you feel obliged to disclose intimate matters of your own, not knowing that the psychopath can use them to blackmail you or to taint your name later on.

For that reason, you need to be wary of a person who opens up to you too quickly after getting acquainted to you the first time; one who is too eager to make you feel like an intimate friend.

Blatant in Stealing Credit

Not only are psychopaths manipulative, they are also extra confident especially when they speak about their accomplishments.

Unfortunately, many of the feats they talk about with pride are non-existent or exaggerated, and often they claim credit that is due to someone else. In fact, the boldness of psychopaths in this regard borders on narcissism.

To shield yourself from falling victim to a psychopath, be alert every time a person delves into his/her successes on no particular basis or completely out of context, especially if those achievements sound special or amazing.

Deliberate Use of a Level Tone

Psychopaths are not known for being animated even when they are speaking of exciting things such as achievements.

Rather, they speak in a slow and low tone and appear to be always calm. The neutrality of their tone ensures they are in full control of what they are letting out of their mouths and communicating to the other person.

This essentially means that the psychopath is keen not to let his/her manner of communication portray his/her true thought process and intention.

If they exhibit any emotions, understand these to be mimicry as they themselves do not have capacity to show compassion.

There is a reason psychopaths find it important to mimic the emotions others manifest, and sometimes even exaggerate them.

It is that people who become emotional after seeing others hurting often catch other people's attention, and psychopaths cannot imagine missing a chance to become the center of attention.

The issue of psychopaths lacking capacity to experience basic emotions has been the subject of several studies, and this deficiency has actually been confirmed by the use of functional magnetic resonance imaging, abbreviated as FMRI.

Psychopaths do not feel remorse or any sense of guilt whatever harm they cause or however ghastly the situation is.

According to one article written for the FBI by Paul Babiak who is an expert in corporate psychopathic behavior, and Mary Ellen who is a forensic behavioral consultant, the only time psychopaths exhibit emotions is when there are people around they want to manipulate.

Unnecessary use of 'because' & 'so that'

You need to keep your guard up when a person's talk is dominated by attempts at justification, as portrayed by the use of 'because' and phrases like 'so that'.

The psychopath speaks in this manner to make it clear there is a cause for what he/she has done, and so you need not make a fuss about the visible effects of his/her action even when they are bad.

Statements of cause-and-effect are common with psychopaths because psychopaths are not prepared to take responsibility for any of their actions.

Unfortunately, unless you appreciate the existence of psychopaths among normal people you could miss this kind of telltale sign, as you are likely to assume the particular words are being used as ordinary conjunctions.

Incidentally, psychopaths often make the cause-and-effect statements even before anyone has thought of accusing them of any wrongdoing.

Some experts from the University of British Columbia are of the same view regarding the cause-and-effect proclamations, explaining that psychopaths use this manner of speaking after they have committed offences to show that what you see, no matter how terrible, is a result of a logical plan.

In fact, according to these experts, psychopaths make it sound as if everyone should be able to appreciate why the results of their actions were inevitable.

Why Psychopaths Often Rise in Leadership

There are many psychopaths within senior management both in government and the private sector, with their percentage being higher than within the general populace.

This is a concern because senior management is where aggrieved employees in lower cadres would expect to find refuge.

Nevertheless, this position should not be surprising because psychopaths have already been known to be egocentric, without empathy, yet charming in a manipulative way; people who have no qualms hurting others on their way up the corporate ladder.

In a December 2019 issue of Forbes, Karen Landay who specialized in business management at the University of Alabama, together with some professors from the University of Iowa, are reported to have noted that psychopaths will stop at nothing to reach the seat of power.

Someone in Your Daily Life Could be a Psychopath

Since whatever is biologically different about the brain of a psychopath does not affect his/her intellect, no arena can preclude the existence of a psychopath. This means you could be working alongside a psychopath irrespective of your profession or business field.

To move up the leadership ladder, individuals need to make a good impression on their superiors, and particularly their immediate supervisors or managers.

With this awareness, the psychopath works towards manipulating these heads on a day-to-day basis, with the aim of getting ahead of other employees.

Ultimately, he/she manages to portray a persona that is entirely false, and on the basis of this deceit he/she is recommended for promotion. Meanwhile, employees who are honest, sincere and good at their work are ignored.

This does not mean the recommending supervisor or manager is incompetent in identifying qualified staff.

On the contrary, he/she will normally have observed all the traits required for promotion such as vision and self-confidence, and he/she will have found those qualities in the psychopath because psychopaths are normally very convincing in their fake mannerisms.

The unfortunate bit is that many employers are yet to realize there are employees highly adept at putting up a show for career promotion, at the expense of more deserving colleagues.

This might explain why an organization may appear to be doing exemplary well financially and otherwise, and then all of a sudden it collapses.

A case in point is the Maxwell business empire that was based in the UK, and which comprised 400 companies spread across the world. The wealth of this empire was reported to have been in billions of sterling pounds.

Maxwell, the business owner, had escaped poverty and risen in social standing from the dangers of Nazi occupation of his motherland, Ukraine – Czechoslovakia at the time – to become a decorated soldier in the British Army and later a Member of Parliament in the UK.

He later entered the publishing business, but because his business successes were based on manipulative deceit, his empire could not withstand honest business practices after his death.

Once the Swiss Bank, one of his creditors, discovered he had sold its loan security without its knowledge, other firms he worked with were prompted to check their positions.

To everyone's dismay, much bigger fraudulent activities were discovered, the most disheartening one being the looting of pension funds that belonged to the empire's employees.

With so many creditors scrambling to be paid the massive debts the business owed them, inevitably the empire came crumbling down.

It is clear from this example that the success of a psychopathic business leader can only continue as long as he/she is actively involved.

It is, therefore, imperative that stakeholders be keen on the kind of CEOs and company directors they choose to lead their organizations, if they want their firms to succeed in perpetuity.

Leadership through Psychopathic Behavior is Untenable

Although people who have used psychopathic tendencies to climb up the career ladder have been termed euphemistically as go-getters, studies have shown that their leadership does not last for long.

Those who acquire leadership status through unscrupulous means and manage to hold onto it for sometime often leave a messy trail behind, as some studies have shown.

One CEO of a UK charity is said to have caused massive staff turnover and a drop in revenues before stakeholders intervened. In short, psychopathic behavior is not a good leadership trait although that has been the misconception in the past.

There was a study done through collaboration between experts from the University of Denver and others from the University of California, Berkeley, which focused on hedge fund managers.

The results showed that hedge fund managers who scored highly in psychopathic behavior played their role more poorly compared to their colleagues whose psychopathic tendencies were much lower.

This conclusion was arrived at after comparing the financial as well as investment returns of the companies the chosen hedge fund managers led from the start of 2005 up to 2015.

Leanne Brinke, a professor of psychology and one who participated in the study, contends that while one may succeed in acquiring power through psychopathic tendencies, this behavior does not help the individual utilize the power at their disposal positively. As such, they are not able to effectively produce the results the company aspires to achieve.

Brinke further elaborates that acquiring power may take intimidation and bullying, but for a manager to succeed in getting excellent results he/she needs to command respect from the people he/she leads.

In the case of the Maxwell business empire, the boss' two sons, Kevin and Ian Maxwell, could not uphold, let alone ride on their father's successes, because the empire had thrived on his own psychopathic traits of manipulation.

In the end, Kevin Maxwell was declared bankrupt to the extent of over 400 million pounds, while Ian was left struggling to pay off debts amounting to half a million pounds.

All in all, while the solution to the problem of psychopaths as characters may be a long time coming, their impact on society can be mitigated if awareness can be raised and everyone is able to detect when a person's behavior feels manipulative and self-serving.

It is also helpful to know the mannerisms that discourage psychopaths from making one a target of manipulation, such as maintaining boundaries and being consistent about it.

Also from the analysis in this book, it is clear that the role of curbing criminal activity by psychopaths cannot be left to the police alone, and that it requires participation of different arms of government.

Criminal lawyers, psychiatric doctors, counselors, researchers, and law enforcement officers should work together with an open mind, with a view to finding a practical solution to the problem of psychopathic behavior.